The Historical and Theological Evolution of Satan, the Devil, and Hell

By Charles River Editors

12th century manuscript illustration depicting Hell

About Charles River Editors

Charles River Editors was founded by Harvard and MIT alumni to provide superior editing and original writing services, with the expertise to create digital content for publishers across a vast range of subject matter. In addition to providing original digital content for third party publishers, Charles River Editors republishes civilization's greatest literary works, bringing them to a new generation via ebooks.

.

Introduction

Medieval fresco depicting Hell

Satan, the Devil, and the History of Hell

The Catholic Church has defined Hell as "a state of definitive self-exclusion from communion with God and the blessed", but the images most have of the Devil and Hell are far more vivid. Even non-Christians are fully familiar with the idea of Hell being a fiery realm of eternal damnation, and the Devil has been depicted so frequently in literature, movies, and television that the figure is instantly recognizable.

While most people know the fairly consistent description of Hell that exists today, the description of Hell has evolved countless times over the centuries, including within the Christian faith. During medieval times, many Christian writers described parts or all of Hell as cold and desolate places, going as far back as the 4th century work *Apocalypse of Paul*. At the same time, the concepts of the Devil and Hell are not unique to Christianity; other major faiths have similar concepts, while ancient religions had an underworld and assorted characters, such as the Greeks' Hades.

Satan, the Devil, and the History of Hell looks at the historical origins of these crucial concepts, as well as the evolution of them over time among Christian and Jewish works, in an effort to trace the history and development of them as central religious tenets. This work includes pictures of historic artwork and a bibliography.

Introductory Note

Oftentimes, tracing the history of a religious idea comes across as either an attempt to disprove that idea or as if starting from the premise that the idea is inherently false, but this is not always the case. Society's most central scientific insights and beliefs have histories that can be traced from periods when no one knew these concepts existed to early, very quaint and strange formulations of these concepts. For example, the existence of the atom is an established fact today, but even before people were truly familiar with it, ancient philosophers were discussing the concept of the atom. Tracing the history of the development of such a concept in no way disparages the existence of the reality behind the concept.

In a similar way, tracing the development of a religious concept is also an exploration of the historical development of an idea, without judgment as to the reality behind the idea itself. Christian theology has coined a term for this idea, calling it "progressive revelation." The idea in Christian theology is that God does not necessarily reveal concepts fully formed but rather reveals them in stages allowing the human mind and the larger community time to process the idea fully. In many cases, when a believer has the opportunity to trace the development of a religious idea, they come to appreciate that idea more fully and to hold it even more dearly than before.

This book traces the history of the development of the Christian personification of evil in figures named variously as Satan, the Devil, Beelzebub, etc. This idea was not fully formed in early Israelite religion, and there are only a handful of references to Satan in the Hebrew Bible; this figure does not appear to be the personification of evil that emerges in Christian theology. Readers of the gospels, however, will find that both Jesus and the Jewish leaders make frequent reference to the devil or Beelzebul, as if everyone around them knows what they are talking about. This apparent jump in conceptual framework is filled in by a significant body of Jewish literature produced in the period between the close of the Hebrew canon in the 4th century B.C. and the ministry of Jesus in the early part of the 1st century A.D. For easy reference, the names these books along with their dates of composition and provenance appear in the chart below:

Title	Original Language	Date	Provenance
Book of the Watchers	Hebrew	300-200 BCE	Palestine
Tobit	Hebrew or Aramaic	225-175 BCE	Palestine
1 Enoch	Hebrew & Aramaic	200 BCE – 100 CE	Judea
Jubilees	Hebrew	160-150 BCE	Palestine
Judith	Hebrew	135-105 BCE	Judea
Apocalypse of Moses [Life of Adam and Eve]	Hebrew	100 BCE - 200 CE	Palestine
Genesis Apocryphon	Aramaic	100 BCE – 100 CE	Palestine
The Wisdom of Solomon	Greek	50-1 BCE	Alexandria, Egypt
4 Maccabees	Greek	20-54 CE	Antioch, Syria
2 Enoch	Greek	50-100 CE	unknown
2 Baruch	Hebrew	75-125 CE	unknown
Apocalypse of Peter	Greek	135 BCE	Egypt

A Broad Overview

Before getting into the details of the development of these religious ideas regarding the "evil one", a broad overview will help provide perspective on the forthcoming journey. The first important point to make is that early Israelite religion was not originally monotheistic but monolotrous; in other words, the earliest layers of the Hebrew Bible both accept and assume the existence of other deities. YHWH, the God of Israel, battles against the deities of other nations and is depicted as taking an exalted position over the other deities.

The Hebrew Bible was not a unified document written at one time from one common perspective but a collection of writings from multiple authors with often quite differing perspectives who lived in radically different time periods. Each writer had a different conception of the world and thus also had different conceptions of God. There are two passages that will help to demonstrate this point clearly. The first is an ancient hymn contained in Deuteronomy 32 that reads:

"When the Most High apportioned the nations,

when he divided humankind,

he fixed the boundaries of the peoples

according to the number of the gods;

YHWH'S own portion was his people,

Jacob his allotted share." (Deut. 32:8-9, NRSV)

In this ancient hymn, the creator God is differentiated from YHWH, the God of Israel. In fact, the creator God stands up and divides humanity into different nationalities with the corresponding political boundaries, a way of acknowledging that each nation has a patron deity who becomes responsible for that group. The idea was that Chemosh became the god of the Moabites and was responsible for them, Baal became the god of the Canaanites, and YHWH was assigned Israel and Judah. Jacob was the father of the twelve tribes of Israel.

This picture of a group of gods headed by the "Most High" also appears in Psalm 82. That psalm reads:

God has taken his place in the divine council;

in the midst of the gods he holds judgment:

'How long will you judge unjustly

and show partiality to the wicked? Selah

Give justice to the weak and the orphan;

maintain the right of the lowly and the destitute.

Rescue the weak and the needy;

deliver them from the hand of the wicked.'

They have neither knowledge nor understanding,

they walk around in darkness;

all the foundations of the earth are shaken.

I say, 'You are gods,

children of the Most High, all of you;

nevertheless, you shall die like mortals,

and fall like any prince.'

Rise up, O God, judge the earth;

for all the nations belong to you!" (Ps. 82, NRSV)

In this psalm, the psalmist paints the picture of a divine assembly of the gods in heaven where the chief God holds court and puts the other gods on trial. The chief deity charges them with neglecting social justice and acting ignorantly, and their punishment for this crime is that they will lose their immortality and become mortal. Rather than each god judging the people to whom he was allotted, the chief creator deity becomes the final arbiter for the people from all nations.

It was not until the Babylonian exile, with the preaching of Isaiah of Babylon (Is. 40-55), that the Israelite religion finally began to embrace monotheism. The concept was relatively new and took awhile to spread throughout the religious community, but by the time the Babylonian exile ended with the Persian conquest of the Babylonians and the subsequent repatriation of the Jews by Darius I, the concept of monotheism had saturated the entire religious community and had become one of the main tenets or hallmarks of Judaism.

The Jews were back in Judah with their monotheistic religion, but during this Persian period, the Jews in Judah had constant interaction with Persian officials, merchants and traders, so interaction between the two sides' religions (Judaism and Zoroastrianism) was inevitable. Zoroastrianism taught a certain dualism in its religious conception. There was God, and then there was the Devil, sometimes called "the Evil One", and these two fought in deadly combat for human loyalty alongside lesser spirits who formed spiritual armies in each respective camp. Spiritual warfare characterized this present age, but the continuous fighting would eventually culminate in one final battle when God would defeat the Devil, destroying him and his demons in a fiery Hell (Riley, 1999, 245).

Naturally, post-exilic Judaism was influenced in many ways by this Zoroastrian model, but it did not borrow all of these ideas wholesale in one fell swoop either. Rather, individual Jewish thinkers during the Hellenistic period borrowed certain elements from this scheme one at a time until the entire model, with a few modifications, became incorporated into the Jewish theological framework.

The Canaanite Astral Revolt Myth

While there is no question that there was a substantial Zoroastrian influence on later Jewish thought, the Hebrew Bible contained many features that readily lent themselves to being placed into this dualistic framework. One such feature was an ancient Canaanite myth regarding a revolt in heaven. The Ugaritic texts found in excavations at Ras Shamra provide firsthand knowledge of this myth, which clearly forms the background to several texts in the Hebrew Bible.

The myth went like this. There was an elderly chief god El who functioned as the creator god and made the rest of the Canaanite pantheon. The most perfect deity created was named Athtar, whom El endowed with great wisdom and beauty. Athtar enjoyed high status on El's mountain (similar to Olympus in Greek mythology) and walked about with the other deities of the pantheon, but he developed a big head and was not content to be second fiddle to the older El. Athtar attempted a coup to take control of the cosmos and the pantheon for himself, claiming to be just as wise as El and to be equal with him in every respect. He sat in El's throne and declared open war against El. However, El defeated him with little difficulty and exiled him from his holy mountain, sentencing him to the underworld (Page, 1990, 222).

The deity Athtar was also connected with Venus. This "star" fascinated ancient astronomers who were unfamiliar with the idea of planets, because unlike the fixed constellations, Venus changed position in the night sky and (more importantly and interestingly to them) disappeared altogether for a time. Ancient observers developed myths to explain the absence of this celestial body from the heavens. In Mesopotamia, the goddess associated with Venus was said to have taken a trip to the netherworld and then escaped ("The Descent of Ishtar"). In Canaanite mythology, this heavenly revolt was the means for understanding the behavior of Venus.

Two of the classical Hebrew prophets made use of this myth in their oracles against kings. Isaiah of Jerusalem used it as the background for an oracle against the king of Babylon (Is. 14:4-

21), and Ezekiel made use of it in two separate oracles against the king of Tyre (Ezek. 28:1-10; 11-19). Later Jewish and Christian interpreters identified these as references to Satan, such as in 'The Birth of Lucifer'.

The Canaanite Prince of the Underworld

In one of the Elijah stories contained in 2 Kings 1, mention is made of the God of Ekron, one of the five Philistine cities. While the actual story itself is incidental and not particularly relevant to the concepts of the Devil and Hell, what is relevant is the intriguing name this deity bears: Baal-zebub. That name, translated in Hebrew or Canaanite (which was spoken by the Philistines at the time), would mean "Lord of the flies." Various Hebrew Bible scholars have attempted to explain the original meaning of this name as either a god who cures diseases, flies as a symbol of solar heat, or the Akkadian parallel "Nintu with the flies" (Herrmann, 1999, 154).

"Beelzebub and them that are with him shoot arrows."

Beelzebub as depicted in John Bunyan's *Pilgrim's Progress*

The current scholarly consensus has turned this interpretation of the name on its head while seeking out how a deity that seems to be named "Lord of the flies" became corrupted to "Beel-zebul" as it appears in the New Testament, where the figure is depicted as the prince or ruler of the demons. Scholars believe that the name found in the Hebrew Bible, "Baal-zebub", is actually a corrupted form of the Canaanite name for the deity, and the idea that Jewish scribed "messed" with the names of Canaanite gods is not far-fetched at all. In actuality, it happened quite a bit, and it most frequently took place with divine elements in personal names, where the names of foreign gods were substituted for words like "shame." According to this narrative, the god's original name was Baal-zebul, which is the proper name "Baal" followed by the epithet "prince", thus forming the name Prince Baal. This then would be a shortened version of the longer title found in the Canaanite mythical texts found at Ugarit. The full form of the name was *Baal-zebul-artz* or "Baal, Prince of the underworld." This name tracks precisely with the context in which this name appears in the New Testament.

Whereas in the case of the astral revolt myth, which has several literary allusions to the myth scattered throughout the prophecies of different Old Testament prophets, there are no such allusions to whatever myth circulated concerning this Canaanite deity. But it seems clear that in Hellenistic Judaism, this myth was well-known, and people identified this deity as the Prince of the Underworld and the leader of the demons. However, the scribes who copied the Hebrew text of kings then amended the consonants contained in this deity's name from *zbl* to *zbb*. In so doing, they demoted this deity from the "Prince of the Underworld" to merely the "Lord of the Flies." But even as the name of the deity was transformed from being "Baal, Prince of the underworld" in Canaanite texts to "Lord of the flies" in the Hebrew Bible, the context of the deity as a prince of the underworld survived to the New Testament.

The Underworld in the Hebrew Bible

The idea of an underworld is at least several thousands of years old, as anyone familiar with ancient civilizations knows. The ancient Egyptian and Mesopotamian religions had grandiose descriptions of the underworld and the journeys of individuals after death, as embodied by the elaborate funeral rituals for the pharaohs and the art and artifacts found in their tombs.

The Hebrew Bible also described an underworld as an abode of the dead, but the picture is much less developed in the Hebrew Bible than in the aforementioned religious traditions. The most frequent term used for the underworld was "sheol," but there was also "the pit," "earth," and "death." Sheol was a watery, deep dark place with gates and bars like a prison that individuals enter but from which no one comes out. Those who dwelt in sheol were called the rephaim.

In the Hebrew Bible, sheol was the destination of all who died. There was no differentiation between the righteous and the unrighteous after death. It was not viewed as a punishment for sin, and there was no fire and no eternal torment. It was simply a murky, opaque existence. But by the late 1st century B.C., fire was introduced to the world of sheol. In the Thanksgiving Hymns composed at Qumran, the hymn identified as Hymn 2 contains the following passage: "[For] the foundations of the mountains [shall quake], fire [shall burn] in Sheol below and [You shall…]" (1 QHª col. 4 line 25)

Having described the Israelite conception of the underworld, the term that will later be translated as Gehenna and used as a term for "hell" deserves at least a passing nod. On the outskirts of Jerusalem, between the border of what were the tribal allotments of Benjamin and Judah, there was a valley known formally as the "valley of the son(s) of Hinnom" (2 Kgs. 23:10; Jer. 7:31). The name was later shortened to simply the "valley of Hinnom" (Neh. 11:30), and the transliteration of this abbreviated phrase is gē-hinnōm. Since the Greek language does not have the phoneme "h" except at the beginning of a word (when it is still not written), Greek writers transliterated this as geenōm, with a breath or glottal stop understood between the two epsilons. The final -ōm was incorrectly analyzed as a plural ending and replaced with a Greek feminine singular ending producing geena or geenē.

For some reason, this valley became the place in ancient Israel for burning bodies. In the monarchic period it was the site of the Tophet, where the worshippers of Molech would sacrifice infant children with fire.[i] The prophet Jeremiah uttered prophecies against this cultic place and against the people who worshipped there, but the punishments Jeremiah pronounced simply involved the death of these worshippers and the desecration of their dead bodies (Jer. 7:29-34; 19:6-9; 32:35). In the Maccabean period, the Maccabees used this valley to burn the corpses of their enemies. The medieval Rabbi David Kimchi (ca. 1200) argued that the valley of Gehenna was an ancient garbage dump where the inhabitants of Jerusalem burned their rubbish continually (Commentary on Psalm 27), but despite the fact that scholars continually cite Kimchi's comments as though they were fact, there is no literary or archaeological support for the idea that the valley was actually used as a garbage dump (Bailey, 1986, 189).

Franz Cumont argued that Christian conceptions of Hell as place of fiery torment was dependent upon Zoroastrian influence (Cumont, 1949, 219-34), and part of the argument hinged on the Zoroastrian picture of the punishment of the dead by molten metal (Yasna 31.3; 51.9). However, closer evaluation has demonstrated that this molten metal was intended to serve a refining, purgatorial purpose rather than the punishing purpose that the fire of Hell has come to serve (Watson, 1992, 927). More recently, Stausberg has examined the Zoroastrian primary materials from a chronological perspective and finds no references to fire associated with hell (Stausberg, 2009, 218).[ii] Similarly, the Greek conception of Hades does not involve fire but is similar to the description of sheol provided above.

The Day of YHWH and Divine Judgment

In the later apocalyptic conceptions, the devil and his demons continue to cause mischief and strife on the earth until the final Day of Judgment. This final Day of Judgment has antecedents in the prophetic writings within the Hebrew Bible itself, and the term the Hebrew prophets used for this day was the "Day of YHWH." Such a day was variously pictured as a day of judgment and a day of redemption.

However, the Day of Judgment was a far cry from modern society's understanding of the Day of Judgment, in which individuals are judged by God and end up in Heaven or Hell. Several prophets proclaimed that various foreign nations would be judged on the Day of YHWH, including Micah, Amos, Hosea and Isaiah, to name a few. The Hebrew prophets also declared that Israel and Judah would be punished on the Day of YHWH (Hos. 11:5; Amos 3:9-11; Is. 5:26-30). In such cases, the punishment or judgment of YHWH identifies groups as a whole, and the punishment envisioned by these prophets is typically military defeat or political subjugation.

Michelangelo's *The Last Judgment*

Satan and the Personification of Evil in the Hebrew Bible

When the Hebrew prophets do touch on individual ethical and moral accountability, they talk in terms of proverbial blessings and curses whose results are assumed to take place during the individual's lifetime. A paradigmatic text in this regard is Ezekiel 18, in which Ezekiel provides an extended oracle emphasizing individual responsibility. The result of living a morally repugnant life is that that life will be cut short; it is not until the latter part of the 2nd century B.C. that readers find the righteous separated from the wicked in "The Separation of the Righteous from the Wicked".

In the story of "the Fall" narrated in the book of Genesis, there is a serpent who deceives Eve into disobeying YHWH, but nowhere does the story itself identify this serpent as "Satan" or the "devil." Some early Jewish interpreters (Philo and Josephus) maintained that the serpent was merely a snake that could talk and walked around on four legs, and they surmised the rest of the animals must have also had this ability of speech in the Garden of Eden.

Later Jewish interpreters began identifying the serpent as Satan or the devil in the 1st century B.C. In the Apocryphal book of the Wisdom of Solomon, there is a roundabout reference to identifying the serpent as "Satan" where the text reads: "for God created us for incorruption, and made us in the image of his own eternity, but through the devil's envy death entered the world, and those who belong to his company experience it" (Wis. 2:23-24, NRSV). This interpretation is even less ambiguous in the Greek Life of Adam and Eve, known as the Apocalypse of Moses, where Eve says, "the devil answered me through the mouth of the serpent" (Apocalypse of Moses 16:4; 17:4). And in 2 Enoch there is the statement, "The devil is of the lowest places...and that is why he thought up the scheme against Adam. In such form he entered paradise and corrupted Eve." (2 Enoch 31:4-6) This connection was already likely current when the author of the New Testament Book of Revelation made the connection between "the ancient serpent, who is the Devil and Satan" (Rev. 12:9; 20:2).

A 12ᵗʰ century stained glass window depicting Adam, Eve, and the Serpent in Saint-Julien cathedral, Le Mans, France.

However, long before this association with Satan was made, the serpent was simply portrayed as a supernatural trickster figure. Trickster figures are widespread in ancient myths and appear in the form of the Mesopotamian Enki, the Greek Prometheus, and the Nordic figure Loki. These figures often mediate between the divine and human realm, and their wily character has given them staying power in the human imagination. The serpent in Genesis 3 is best thought of in this category.

The Hebrew word "*śatan*" appears multiple times in the Hebrew Bible with two distinct but related meanings. The first meaning is that of an "opponent." This could be an opponent in battle, as when the Philistines use it to describe David when they are unwilling to fight alongside him for fear that he will turn on them as "a *śatan*" and slit their throats (1 Sam 29:4). The term is also used for the military opponents of Solomon, Hadad (1 Kings 11:14, 25) and Rezon (1 Kings 11:23). It could also be used in a political or social context (Ps. 38:20).

In two of the four contexts where this term refers to a supernatural being, it has this first meaning. The first is the story of Balaam and his ass. Balaam was a prophet of YHWH and visionary from a foreign country who was summoned by Balak, the king of Moab, to prophesy for him regarding his impending battle with the Israelites (Num 22:4-6). The first time the messengers summoned Balaam, he refused to go with them because of the message he received from YHWH (Num. 22:7-14). The second time they pled with him, he consulted YHWH yet again and this time was given the green light (Num. 22:15-21). In one of the most interesting theological passages in the Hebrew Bible, God becomes angry with Balaam for following his explicit instructions (Num. 22:22), and in an inexplicable fit of rage, God sends the angel of YHWH to Balaam to act as "a *śatan*," or an opponent against Balaam (Num. 22:22, 32). This angel acts as a divine toll keeper, not allowing Balaam to pass until he has spoken with YHWH (Num. 22:23-35). This amusing tale has many baffling aspects, including why YHWH reiterates the exact same message to Balaam as he had received in his dream the night before, but the function and role of the angel of YHWH, acting as "a *śatan*" in this story, is quite clear.

Rembrandt's painting, *Balaam and his Ass*.

The second context appears in the Chronicler's retelling of an incident during the reign of David. While several scholars connect the meaning of "*śatan*" in this context with its second meaning identified below, Stokes (2009) makes a compelling argument for interpreting its meaning in light of the Balaam story. Interpreters of the Hebrew Bible from ancient times to the present have recognized that the Chronicler is retelling the material from Samuel and Kings using his own theological framework. In order to understand what the Chronicler is doing, it is best to begin with a summary of the account in 2 Samuel 24.

In the narrative, YHWH becomes angry with Israel and commands David to take a census of the people (2 Sam. 24:1. David then asks Joab, the commander of his army, to conduct the census (2 Sam. 24:2). Joab initially questions the motives behind the king's request, but he eventually complies with the order (2 Sam. 24:3-9). However, David then cries out and repents to YHWH for doing exactly what YHWH had commanded him to do (2 Sam. 24:10).

Through the seer named Gad, YHWH then offers three alternatives that David and Israel can receive as punishment: three years of famine, three months of being routed by his enemies in battle, or three days of pestilence throughout the land (2 Sam. 24:11-13). David requests that the punishment take the form of either the first or third option, and YHWH decides on option number three and kills 70,000 in Israel (2 Sam. 24:15). But as the angel is about to destroy Jerusalem itself, YHWH himself repents of his "evil" decision (that's what the text says) and stops the angel of destruction before he lays waste to Jerusalem (2 Sam. 24:16). David then purchases a location for a sacrificial altar, makes a sacrifice and thereby stops the plague from spreading any further throughout the land (2 Sam. 24:18-25).

Stokes highlights five different connections between the Balaam account in Numbers 22 and the original story concerning David and the census contained in 2 Samuel 24. In both accounts: 1) the deity's anger was kindled; 2) the angel of YHWH goes forth to execute judgment; 3) the main characters confess their sin when they see the angel of YHWH; 4) the deity instructs the main characters in how to avert impending disaster; and 5) the deity instructs the main character to act and then becomes angry or lashes out when they comply with the deity's explicit instructions (Stokes, 2009, 101-2). Because of these many points of connection between the two stories, it would be natural for ancient interpreters to read one story in light of the other. The Chronicler read both of these stories in light of each other, and incorporating an additional connection with the term "*śatan*" that had been limited to the Balaam account would be entirely natural. The Chronicler saw the actions of YHWH inciting David to count the people as being parallel to the figure that blocked Balaam's path. If so, the term "*śatan*" is not a proper noun in this example, as many translators have rendered it, but rather a common noun to explain "an opponent rose against Israel…" (1 Chr. 21:1)

Before moving on to the other meaning of the word "*śatan*," there is another term that appears in both the Chronicles (1 Chr. 21:15) and the Samuel (2 Sam. 24:16) account regarding David and the census that warrants discussion. It is the adjective that is used to describe the angel that carries out the devastation wrought by the plague: destroying. If this were the only occurrence of this word connected with an angel, it would probably not be very noteworthy. Only a couple of phrases earlier, this word appears in its verbal form describing the action the angel is about to undertake: "But when the angel stretched out his hand toward Jerusalem to destroy it…" (2 Sam. 24:16). However, the author of the Exodus account of the ten plagues against Egypt uses this same word, standing alone as a noun, to describe the agent of God who carries out the death of the Egyptian firstborn males (Ex. 12:23).

The parallels between these two agents are just as close as the parallels between this story and the account of Balaam and his ass. In the narrative report of the census, the description of the pestilence begins with "So YHWH sent a pestilence on Israel from that morning until the appointed time…" (2 Sam. 24:15). Similarly, the plague narrative begins, "Thus says YHWH, 'About midnight I will go out through Egypt. Every firstborn in the land of Egypt shall die…'" (Ex. 11:4-5). In both cases, it is YHWH who will bring the destruction. In both accounts, the destroying angel appears at the last minute to actually carry out the deed.

In terms of a possible corollary for this figure in human society, one might think of the relationship between the king and his executioner. The king is the only one with the authority to pass down a death sentence and is the ultimate cause of any death so ordered. On the other hand, the king never gets his hands dirty by actually killing anyone. This unsavory task is relegated to a member of the royal court, who is handsomely rewarded for his service. This conceptualization is most likely what lies behind this figure in these two texts. The deity makes the ultimate decision concerning life or death, but the death sentence is carried out by an underling to whom the job has been relegated.

When the Hebrew term "śatan" does not mean opponent in general, it has a more specific meaning, namely that of a legal opponent or prosecuting attorney. The clearest instance of this appears in Psalm 109, where the text reads:

> "They encircle me with words of hate;
>
> They attack me without cause.
>
> They answer my love with accusation
>
> and I must stand judgment…
>
> Appoint a wicked man over him;
>
> may an accuser (śatan) stand at his right side;
>
> may he be tried and convicted;
>
> may he be judged and found guilty." (Ps. 109:4-7, NJPS)

The hypothetical setting envisioned by the psalmist is that of a courtroom trial. In the first part, the psalmist laments that those whom he loved and to whom he showed kindness have repaid him by putting him on trial. His petition of God then is that there would be a reversal of fortune, and that the one who formerly accused (a verbal form of the word śatan) him would be forced to stand trial himself. In the psalmist's vision, this individual would be forced to face a similar "wicked" prosecuting attorney, or "accuser", as the psalmist has to face. This psalm is especially interesting in this context because it identifies the spatial position of the prosecuting attorney in the courtroom, as he stands to the right of the accused. Later on in the psalm, there is another nugget that seems to provide information about the courtroom proceedings in ancient Israel. The psalmist says, "My accusers shall be clothed in shame, wrapped in their disgrace as with a robe." (Ps. 109:29, NJPS). This verse indicates that the accused was often wearing clothing that marked him out as a criminal. This would be similar sociologically to the orange jumpsuit that some individuals wear when they are arraigned.

In the remaining three instances where the term *śatan* refers to a supernatural being, it has this legal connotation. Many of the Hebrew prophets and the psalmists picture a divine courtroom with many of the same functions of the Israelite courtroom, albeit reflected in the divine realm. The role of the *śatan* appears clearly in two of these spiritual contexts.

The clearest picture of the role of this figure appears in the prophetic book of Zechariah. In the third chapter of the book, Zechariah sees a vision in which the chief priest in Jerusalem, Joshua, is standing before the angel of YHWH. The scene is clearly a heavenly courtroom, where Joshua is on trial and the angel of YHWH is playing the role of the divine judge. "The *śatan*" is standing in the position of the courtroom at the right of the accused, occupied by the prosecuting attorney ready to accuse Joshua. Then suddenly, the courtroom proceeding is interrupted by a shout, as YHWH himself appears in the courtroom and rebukes the prosecuting attorney for even bringing this case to trial. After the interruption, the judge, the angel of YHWH, has the bailiff remove Joshua's filthy and stained clothes and replace them with clean party clothes. This would be akin to removing the orange jumpsuit in the middle of the courtroom and replacing it with a fancy suit and tie. The judge then passes a verdict in the case, declaring, "See, I have taken your guilt away from you…" (Zech. 3:4, NRSV). It is clear by the angel's very statement that Joshua, the high priest, was guilty of some crime that warranted the action on the part of the prosecuting attorney, and it is only the intervention of YHWH into the court proceedings that saves Joshua from his deserved punishment.

This same picture forms the background to the book of Job. In the book of Job, YHWH takes the time to converse with the divine prosecuting attorney, "the Satan." He informs YHWH that he has been moving about the earth, undoubtedly looking for cases of injustice to prosecute. YHWH, pleased with the lack of such cases, takes the opportunity to point out one exceedingly righteous individual. The prosecuting attorney's reply is not that YHWH has protected Job from himself, because this role, later played by Satan, does not belong to this figure. When he suggests that adversity has not fallen upon Job, the alternative he suggests is that YHWH should stretch out his hand to create adversity for Job. From a later apocalyptic perspective, one would expect the conversation to have been for YHWH to lower the fence around Job so that he, Satan, could inflict hardship and trial on the person of Job. But this later perspective is not the perspective of the author of Job.

Sociologists and anthropologists have found that the idea of demon possession is common to most primitive societies, and the clearest picture of demon possession in the Hebrew Bible appears with King Saul. In the Saul narrative contained in 1 Sam 16-19, at various points mention is made of an "evil spirit" that overcomes and torments Saul. This evil spirit causes Saul physical pain that can be soothed by music. The evil spirit also causes Saul to rave within his house and gives him murderous impulses; at one point, Saul takes the spear within his hand and hurls it at David. This general picture of madness brought about by demon possession is typical of the picture of demon possession that emerges in the New Testament.

In this Rembrandt painting, David plays music for Saul

From Hebrew to Greek

In the Hellenistic period in Palestine (as it was known at the time), Jewish communities were faced with a difficult problem. Their religious texts were written in Hebrew, but Hebrew was no longer spoken in the region as a native language. The scribes and religious scholars still knew and studied the language, but the language had nearly died out and was becoming much more inaccessible to the common religious Jews who wanted access to the sacred texts. As Alexander the Great pushed the translation of various sacred and otherwise important documents from other languages into Greek throughout his empire, the Hebrew Bible became a logical choice for such a task.

Beginning around the 3rd century B.C., bilingual scholars began working on translating the books of the Hebrew Bible. However, as they went about their work, their changes affected how certain parts of the text read. For example, the Greek word *diabolos*, which the translators of the Septuagint chose to use for the word "*śatan*", has a more restricted semantic range than the original Hebrew term. The Hebrew term, as has been described above, had the general sense of accusing or opposing someone, and the accusation, as in the legal sense, can be either legitimate or illegitimate. Conversely, the Greek word *diabolē* means specifically a "false accusation or slander" (Liddell & Scott, 1994, 159), and the related substantive version of the word, *diabolos*, thus means a "false accuser or slanderer." The Greek translators of the Septuagint made an interpretive decision by using this term for the Hebrew term "*śatan*", and obviously the Greek term puts a negative spin on any of the figures so described. It is this Greek term that entered English as "devil."

The Christian scholar Jerome, who was primarily responsible for the Latin translation of the Hebrew Bible in the 4th century A.D., took it one step further. In certain passages where the Hebrew term "*śatan*" appeared (Job 1, 1 Chr. 21; Zech 3), Jerome retained this Hebrew word as if it were a proper name, thereby making the name Satan. But in other passages, he translated the actual meaning of the word with terms like adversarer and adversarium, meaning "adversary" (Num. 22; 1 Kgs. 11). This translation technique served to impose the later New Testament and Jewish Apocalyptic perspective onto the Hebrew Bible.

Bartolomeo Cavarozzi's painting of St. Jerome

The Creation of Demons and their Leader

One of the major problems preventing Jewish thinkers from adopting the Zoroastrian conceptualization of the Devil and demons was the question of their origin. In the Zoroastrian worldview, God and the Devil were two eternal opposing forces who each created for themselves an army of lesser divine beings to fight alongside them. Such a conceptualization was incongruent with the thoroughgoing monotheism that characterized post-exilic Jewish thought.

The first step in developing the concept of a being who personified evil and opposed God was to develop an origin myth that explained how such a being came into existence in the first place. The Hebrew Bible is replete with references to angels, and Jewish scholars had no problem incorporating their creation into the creation account given in Genesis 1. The book of Jubilees seamlessly incorporates the creation of the angels into the account:

> "For on the first day he created the heavens, which are above, and the earth, and
> the waters and all of the spirits which minister before him:
>
> the angels of the presence,

and the angels of sanctification,

and the angels of the spirit of fire,

and the angels of the spirit of the winds,

and the angels of the spirit of the clouds and darkness and snow

and hail and frost,

and the angels of resoundings and thunder and lightning,

and the angels of the spirits of cold and heat and winter and

springtime and harvest and summer,

and all of the spirits of his creatures which are in heaven and on

earth." (Jub. 2:2)

However, a devil and demons could not be easily fit into such a schema, because the creation account specifically indicates that all of God's creation was "good." The personification and embodiment of evil could certainly not be called good, so this "evil one" could not have been part of the initial creation.

The Jewish scholars found a source for this myth in an obscure passage surrounding Noah and the flood account. The passage reads as follows: "When men began to increase on earth and daughters were born to them, the divine beings (lit. 'sons of God') saw how beautiful the daughters of men were and took wives from among those that pleased them...It was then, and later too, that the Nephilim appeared on earth—when the divine beings cohabitated with the daughters of men, who bore them offspring. They were the heroes of old, the men of renown." (Gen. 6:1-4)

As it stands, this passage originally recorded a Hebrew tradition about demigods, akin to Hercules in Greek tradition or Gilgamesh in Sumerian lore. But such original intention did not concern ancient interpreters; here was a story that allowed the Jewish writers to talk of demons as "fallen angels." In this way, the "fall" of the angels was akin to the "fall" of humanity in the Garden of Eden.

The author of the Book of the Watchers, which became embedded in 1 Enoch, elaborated on this tale at great length. It begins by retelling the passage from Genesis cited above, but it specifically identifies the "children of heaven" as angels. These angels then lusted after the human women and wanted to mate with them. Their leader, named Semyaz, expressed concern that, as their leader, he alone will be held responsible for the actions of this group of angels. 200

angels in all swear an oath (curse) that they will carry out this plan. They copulate with the human women, and these women bear giants from these unions.

The passage in Genesis does specifically indicate that these Nephilim were the offspring of the divine and human unions, but the implication is clear. Early interpreters connected this enigmatic passage in Genesis with the only instance where the term Nephilim occurs. In the book of Numbers, in a report that the spies bring back from the land of Canaan, they make the following remark: "All the people that we saw in it are men of great size; we saw the Nephilim there—the Anakites are part of the Nephilim—and we looked like grasshoppers to ourselves, and so we must have looked to them." (Num. 13:32-33). The connection between these two passages and the identification of the Nephilim in the Genesis account as giants is ancient and goes back to the 3rd century B.C. with the Greek translation of the Torah, where the Septuagint translates Genesis 6:4 as follows: "Now the giants were on the earth in those days and afterwards." (Pietersma, 2007, 9).

Returning to the narrative, these giants then ate all of the people's food and even became cannibals. The three chief angels, Michael, Surafel, and Gabriel, then look down from heaven and observe the suffering being inflicted by the giants. They obtain an audience with God and point out to him the group of beings that has taught the humans "eternal secrets." They also point out Semyaz and his group of rebellious angels. God sends one angel to inform Noah of the impending flood and tells another angel, Raphael, to bind Azazel, the leader of those who taught the arts and sciences to the humans, and to throw him into a pit where he will stay awaiting the fire at the great Day of Judgment. God then declares that his angels are to kill the giants, and God also declares that Semyaz and his Watchers are to be thrown into prison until the day of eternal judgment.

The narrative then takes a radical turn and begins to focus on a figure called Enoch. This figure is said to have lived with the Watchers and the angels. Enoch intercedes for Azazel and reprimands the Watchers. He then experiences a grand vision, and it is in this vision that the origin and nature of "evil spirits" is revealed to the reader. First, Enoch sees a vision of the almighty God described in tremendously flowery detail. God then speaks to Enoch and explains that evil spirits have emerged from the bodies of the giants. They are spiritual beings, but distinct from angels, who are spiritual beings of heaven. These are spirits of earth, because they were born on earth. As spirits, they do not need to eat or drink. These evil spirits will continue to corrupt humanity until the final Day of Judgment.

In Jubilees, the picture is slightly different. The name of the leader of these fallen angels is Mastema, or Beliar. In four instances, the name of the leader is given as Satan. The reason they leave heaven in the first place is not lust but to teach humans about justice and righteousness. It is only once they are among the humans that find themselves lusting after the human women and copulate with them. But in Jubilees, rather than being thrown into the pit to await eternal judgment, Mastema pleas with God to allow him to keep only a tenth of his fallen angels, who will continue to plague humanity until the end of time.

A medieval woodcutting depicting Belial

Hell as a Place of Fire and Torment

After that vision, the angels take Enoch on a tour of the earth. On this journey, Enoch rides into various natural phenomena, gaining a perspective on weather events like tornados and lightning. Enoch is also shown the place where the waters of all the seas flow (they did not yet have a concept of a spherical earth). Enoch then flies to the west, where there are seven mystical mountains made of precious stones. It is inside this mountain range of precious stones that Enoch sees what would today be called Hell. It is the prison for those who rebelled against the commandments of God. He describes the place as follows:

> "And I saw a deep pit with heavenly fire on its pillars; I saw inside them descending pillars of fire that were immeasurable (in respect to both) altitude and depth. And on top of that pit I saw a place without the heavenly firmament above it or earthly foundation under it or water. There was nothing on it—not even birds—but it was a desolate and terrible place...(Then) the angel said (to me), 'This place is the (ultimate) end of heaven and earth: it is the prison house for the stars and the powers of heaven...Here shall stand in different appearances the angels which have united themselves with women.'" (1 En. 18:11-14)

In a subsequent vision, Enoch sees another place identified similarly as the prison for the rebellious angels:

"I then proceeded from that area to another place which is even more terrible and saw a terrible thing: a great fire that was burning and flaming; the place had a cleavage (that extended) to the last sea, pouring out great pillars of fire; neither its extent nor its magnitude could I see nor was I able to estimate. At that moment, what a terrible opening 'is this place and a pain to look at!' Then Ura'el, (one) of the holy angels who was with me, responded and said to me, 'Enoch, why are you afraid like this?' (I answered and said), 'I am frightened because of this terrible place and the spectacle of this painful thing.' And he said unto me, 'This place is the prison house of the angels; they are detained here forever.' (1 En. 21:7-10)

One can witness the gradual development of these ideas in the Hellenistic period. In the late 2nd century B.C. book of Judith, the day of judgment now involves three features that will become hallmarks of hell: fire, weeping, and worms. The relevant passage reads:

"Woe to the nations that rise up against my people!

The Lord Almighty will take vengeance on them in the day of

judgment;

he will send fire and worms into their flesh;

they shall weep in pain forever." (Judith 16:17)

This statement in Judith shows some literary dependence on a passage in Isaiah: "And they shall go out and look at the dead bodies of the people who have rebelled against me; for their worm shall not die, their fire shall not be quenched, and they shall be an abhorrence to all flesh" (Is. 66:24). In the prophecy found in Isaiah, the statement about worms and fire is clearly related to the treatment of their corpses, which are defiled in these ways. In Judith, however, these elements take on the character of a final judgment of people. But it is also important to note that the punishment in Judith is still corporate in its perspective; the recipients of these future punishments are not yet wicked individuals but rather the nations that oppose Israel and Judah.

In 2 Baruch, the following passage appears:

"For behold, the Most High will cause all these things to come. There will not be an opportunity to repent anymore, nor a limit to the times, nor a duration of the periods, nor a change to rest, nor an opportunity to prayer, nor sending up petition, nor giving knowledge, nor giving love, nor opportunity of repentance, nor supplicating for offenses, nor prayers of the fathers, nor intercessions of the prophets, nor help of the righteous. There is the proclamation of judgment to corruption, regarding the way to the fire and the path that leads to the glowing coals." (2 Bar. 85:12-15)

The Separation of the Righteous from the Wicked

After touring these two hellish places, Enoch travels to yet another place, where beautiful corners have been dug out of the precious stones that make up the mountains. It is in these "beautiful corners" that the spirits of the souls of the dead reside. The angel then explains to Enoch how the souls are separated:

> "At that moment, I raised a question regarding him and regarding the judgment of all, 'For what reason is one separated from the other?' And he replied and said to me, 'These three have been made in order that the spirits of the dead might be separated. And in the manner in which the souls of the righteous are separated (by) this spring of water with light upon it, in like manner, the sinners are set apart when they die and are buried in the earth and judgment has not been executed upon them in their lifetime, upon this great pain, until the great day of judgment— and to those who curse (there will be) plague and pain forever, and the retribution of their spirits. They will bind them there forever—even if from the beginning of the world. And in this manner is a separation made for the souls of those who make the suit (and) those who disclose concerning destruction, as they were killed in the days of the sinners. Such has been made for the souls of the people who are not righteous, but sinners and perfect criminals; they shall be together with (other) criminals who are like them, (whose) souls will not be killed on the day of judgment but will not rise from there.'" (1 En. 22:8-13)

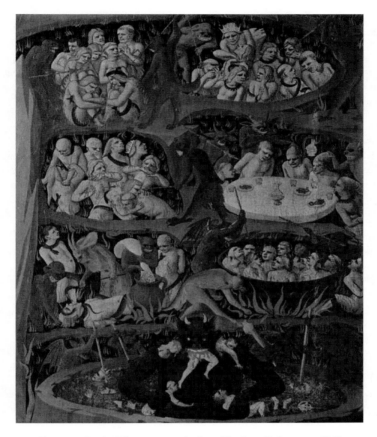

Fra Angelico's 15th century painting, *The Last Judgement, Hell*

Demon Possession in Hellenistic and Roman Literature

The Apocryphal/Deutero-canonical book of Tobit provides one of the earliest stories of demonic exorcism in Jewish literature. The book describes a woman named Sarah, living in Media, who had walked down the aisle with seven men. After they would say their nuptials and enter the bedchamber, the men would wind up dead before the marriage could be consummated. The narrator explains that a wicked demon named Asmodeus was the one responsible for the death of these men, but the woman's maid had a different interpretation of the situation and accused Sarah of murdering each of her husbands. The combination of these two perspectives leads the reader to the conclusion that Sarah was possessed by the demon Asmodeus and would become filled with murderous rage (similar to the case of King Saul) whenever she would enter her bedchamber with a new husband.

The main character of the story, Tobias, is to be Sarah's eighth husband. An angel appears to Tobias and provides him with a prescription for exorcising the demon. Azariah, the angel, instructs him to remove the heart and liver from a fish. He is then to burn these in the bedchamber, and the resulting smoke will drive out the demon from his new wife.

Josephus, a Jewish historian, describes how a fellow Jew named Eleazar performed an exorcism using similar olfactory methods (Antiquities VIII 46-48). Using a prescription handed down by Solomon, Eleazar held a type of smelling salt under the nose of the man who was possessed. The man inhaled the concoction and passed out. Eleazar then proceeded to chant various incantations, ordering the demon out of the man. In order to prove to a group of observers that the demon had indeed left the man, Eleazar set up a small washbasin with water some distance from the man. Eleazar then ordered the demon to depart from the man and to tip over the basin of water.

Another description of demonic possession from around the time of the apostle Paul's ministry appears in the writings of Plutarch. Plutarch describes the case of a man named Nicias who threw himself upon the ground in the middle of a speech and then lifted his head and spoke in strange haunting tones (Plutarch, *Lives*, *Marcellus* 20.5). He then stripped himself naked and ran around, screaming that he thought he was being chased by mothers. The term Plutarch uses to describe his behavior is δαιμονῶτι ("possessed by demons").

The idea that Satan or one of his demons could possess someone is reflected at Qumran, where there is an apotropaic prayer for protection. It reads, "Do not let Satan or an unclean spirit rule over me; do not let pain or an evil inclination take possession of my bones." (11Q5 19.15-16). This prayer from the Psalms Scroll at Qumran demonstrates that 1st century Jews in Palestine believed that both Satan and other demons could take possession of one's body and cause them to do evil things.

One additional story about demon possession and affliction appears in the *Genesis Apocryphon* found at Qumran. This text is a retelling of the stories of the patriarchs. This popular type of literature was a way to update the Biblical stories and make them more relevant to their contemporary audience. Along the way, the storytellers resolved and smoothed over any theological or other problems that they encountered in the original Biblical text. One problem storytellers wrestled with was the account of the patriarch Abraham, who passed his wife Sarah off as his sister, along with the fact that his sister married the pharaoh for a time because of this ruse (Gen 12:10-20). The Biblical text implies that the pharaoh actually married Sarah and presumably had sexual intercourse with her. The idea that this would take place, and that Abraham would then take his wife Sarah back after she had slept with another man, was morally repugnant to many Jewish readers.

As an answer to this moral dilemma, the storytellers behind the *Genesis Apocryphon* came up with the following solution. Abraham prayed desperately to God the night pharaoh took his wife that the pharaoh would somehow not defile his wife (1QapGen col. 20 lines 10-16). God answered Abraham's prayer by sending a "baleful spirit" upon pharaoh that made him and every man of his household impotent (1QapGen col. 20 lines 16-21). Therefore, the plague that pharaoh experienced recorded in the original Biblical account (Gen. 12:17) was a plague of impotence brought on by demon possession.

Satan in the Christian Tradition

Depiction of Satan in Dante's *Inferno*

Jesus was born into a Hellenistic Jewish society, and accounts of his life and work reflect many of the customs and beliefs of Hellenistic Jews at that time. Part of the cultural inheritance that he received involved beliefs about Satan and Hell, which is made clear by various sayings of Jesus recorded in the canonical gospels and elsewhere. In fact, scholars have noted that exorcism was one of the most frequent elements in Christ's ministry, at least according to the earliest accounts.

In the earliest gospel, Mark (ca. 70 A.D.), Jesus refers to Satan in three different sayings. In the first story of interest, Jesus is visiting his hometown in the region of Galilee when the "unclean spirits" make obeisance to Jesus and shout out, "You are the Son of God" (Mark 3:11). This is part of the overarching theme of Mark's gospel, which is the Messianic secret. Throughout Mark's gospel, the demons are the only ones who proclaim Christ's identity as the "Son of God", and he always silences them when they do so. When Jesus travels from the sea to his actual hometown of Nazareth, the crowd begins to whisper that Jesus has gone mad, and his family tries to restrain him. The scribes then accuse him of being possessed by Beelzebul, by whose authority he casts out demons (Mark 3:22). This accusation results in the following parable from the lips of Jesus:

> "How can Satan cast out Satan? If a kingdom is divided against itself, that kingdom cannot stand. And if a house is divided against itself, that house will not be able to stand. And if Satan has risen up against himself and is divided, he cannot stand, but his end has come. But no one can enter a strong man's house and plunder his property without first tying up the strong man; then indeed the house can be plundered." (Mark 3:23-27)

According to Mark, although other Jews of his time used the term "Beelzebul" for the "prince of the demons", Jesus preferred the native Hebrew term "Satan." The second instance where Jesus refers to Satan in his preaching is in the parable of the sower. Jesus first tells a crowd a parable about a man who sows seeds on various types of soil. When he is alone, the 12 Disciples ask him to explain the meaning of his parable. It is in this private context that Jesus explains that within the parable, the birds who snatch away the seeds from the rocky soil represent "Satan" (Mark 3:15), "the evil one" (Matt. 13:19), or "the devil" (Luke 8:12) snatching away the word of God from people's hearts.

The third instance is where Jesus privately prophesies his death to the 12 disciples, at which point Peter takes Jesus aside to rebuke him for saying such things. To this, Jesus responds abruptly, "Get behind me, Satan." (Mark 8:33, NRSV). Given the exalted role that Peter begins to play in the early church, this passage has often been used as a prime example of the criterion of embarrassment for establishing the historicity of Christ's sayings. Because of the embarrassment involved in Jesus rebuking this leader of the early church so strongly, it seems highly unlikely that the early church would invent such a statement to put into his mouth.

Another instance where Satan appears, not as an element in Christ's preaching but as an actual character in the narrative itself, is when Jesus was tempted in the wilderness for 40 days after his baptism by John. In this scene, Satan is not an unseen evil spirit working behind the scenes but a figure who talks with Jesus and leads Jesus around to various places, including a high mountain and the pinnacle of the temple. The description here is very reminiscent of the scenes in the apocalyptic literature, where an angel or heavenly being appears to the main character and leads him on a tour of the earth or of heaven. Similarly, Christ's interaction with Satan as a conversation is quite similar to the types of question and answer dialogues found in the apocalyptic literature from the Hellenistic period.

THE TEMPTATION OF JESUS

And the devil, taking him up into an high mountain, shewed unto him all the kingdoms of the world in a moment of time... (Luke 4: 5)

Beyond the Gospel of Mark, the other gospel writers mention Satan in some additional contexts in Christ's ministry. The gospel of Luke contains twice or three times as many references to evil spirits as do the other gospel writers. One prominent place where Satan appears in the gospel of Luke is during the commissioning of the 70 (Luke 10:1-20). This commissioning of the 70 does not appear in any other gospel, and in Matthew, the instructions given to the 70 are given instead to the 12. But in Luke, Jesus sends these 70 disciples out in pairs with instructions to heal and to preach the arrival of the Kingdom of God. Upon their return, the 70 are elated and declare, "Lord, in your name even the demons submit to us!" (Luke 10:17). Christ's reply, in which he pictures Satan falling from the sky like a flash of lightning, also sounds reminiscent of the apocalyptic visions. Jesus is seeing as if into another realm where the actions of his disciples cause Satan's defeat.

Another prominent introduction of Satan by Luke is in the account of the betrayal by Judas Iscariot. According to Luke, Judas engaged in his repugnant actions as a result of demonic possession by Satan himself.

Matthew adds his own story about the devil that does not appear in the other gospels. In Matthew, Jesus describes an eschatological picture for his audience. The Son of Man comes with his angels and takes the throne. He then divides the nations who are in front of him in the same way that a shepherd separates the sheep from the goats. The Son of Man gladly welcomes those who engaged in acts of hospitality and social justice into his future kingdom, but he sorely rebukes and chastises those who failed to show hospitality and social justice to others. This clearly reflects the separation of the wicked from the righteous described above, and the Son of Man figure actually begins his rebuke of this latter group with this statement: "You that are accursed, depart from me into the eternal fire prepared for the devil and his angels" (Matt. 25:41).

The Roles Played by Satan in the New Testament

There are various roles that Satan plays in various books that make up the remainder of the New Testament. In most cases, these roles have precedents in either the Hebrew Bible itself or in earlier Jewish literature.

Like the role of the "satan" in the story of Balaam and his ass, Satan serves to block Christians from making certain journeys. In his letter to the Thessalonians, Paul declares that he wanted to come to Thessalonica to visit the church he had planted there, but that Satan blocked him and his companions from making that journey (1 Thess. 2:18).

Another role that Satan plays in the New Testament is that of a deceiver, similar to the equation of Satan with the serpent in the Garden of Eden. In one of Paul's letters to the Corinthian church, he notes that Satan will disguise himself as an angel of light in accordance with this deceptive purpose (2 Cor. 11:14). In the same letter, he refers to an individual who caused a great amount of strife and contention between himself and the Corinthian congregation. He asks the congregation to reassure him that they love and accept him, and that Paul forgives him just as they do. Paul then adds an aside that they do this so that they will not be outwitted by Satan.

Satan also plays the related role of tempter, which also connects with the serpent in the story of

Adam and Eve. In his first letter to the church at Corinth, Paul urges the married couples to not withhold sex from their spouses, except for agreed upon times (1 Cor. 7:5). The reasoning Paul gives for this is that such action will give Satan an opportunity to tempt one or the spouses.

Additionally, there is a clear dualism evident in the New Testament between the Kingdom of God and the Kingdom of Satan. This dualism is not as full-blown as in the Gnostic writings, but it is certainly apparent. In several instances, the apostle Paul mentions turning individuals over to Satan. For example, he instructs the Corinthian congregation to hand over to Satan the man who is now living with his father's wife in sexual immorality. At the end of his letter to the Romans, written at the end of his life, Paul issues the following closing blessing to the church at Rome: "The God of peace will shortly crush Satan under your feet." (Rom 16:20, NRSV). And in the pastoral letter to Timothy, which is also attributed to Paul, the author mentions that he has turned over two individuals to Satan for the sin of blasphemy (1 Tim. 1:20). The author also mentions that some have already turned away in order to follow Satan (1 Tim. 5:15).

One role that seems to be a new element is Satan as tormentor. In one of his letters to the church at Corinth, the apostle Paul makes reference to a physical infirmity he was suffering. The nature of this infirmity has been the source of much speculation amongst scholars, but the important point for is that the apostle describes it as "a messenger of Satan to torment me" (2 Cor. 12:7, NRSV). This idea of Satan as a tormentor only barely surfaces in this New Testament text, but it becomes much more prominent in later Christian tradition.

Satan in The Book of Revelation

Frontpiece of a medieval version of the Book of Revelation

The book of Revelation is the one apocalyptic book in the New Testament, and the name of the book itself (Revelation) is actually the English translation of the Greek word *apokalypsis*. The book begins with messages from the risen Christ to seven different churches throughout the Roman Empire, and the remainder of the book describes an extended vision that John the elder sees while on the island of Patmos. A great deal of the book focuses on the figure of Satan and his demons in a cosmic final battle with God.

Many of the previous themes about Satan and his demons appear together in the book of

Revelation. In chapter 9, there is the first reference to Satan and his demons, but in the preceding chapter (8), different angels have been blowing different trumpets to release various plagues upon the earth. When the fifth angel in the sequence of seven blows his trumpet, a star falls from heaven to earth (recall the references in the book of the Watchers to angels as stars), and this star receives the key to the bottomless pit (Rev. 9:1). He opens the shaft to the bottomless pit, and smoke arises from the shaft, along with locusts (Rev. 9:2-3). These locusts are allowed to torture all of those human beings who have not received the seal of God on their foreheads. They torture these humans as scorpions would, stinging them continually for five months but not killing them (Rev. 9:3-5). John describes their appearance with human faces, women's hair, wings, the teeth of lions, and tails of scorpions. Their leader is the angel of the bottomless pit, called Abaddon or Apollyon. This figure, Abaddon, appears in the Book of the Watchers, where the place of destruction, Abaddon, is personified as an angel with that same name (1 En. 20:2).

Christian and Apollyon.

CHRISTIAN'S COMBAT WITH APOLLYON

An illustration of Apollyon fighting a Christian in John Bunyan's *Pilgrim's Progress*

In chapter 12, the elder John then sees a vision of a great red dragon, who sweeps a third of the stars out of heaven (harkening back to the descriptions of fallen angels in the Book of the Watchers and Jubilees). This picture is not of a future event but summarizes the birth, death and resurrection of Jesus from the standpoint of a cosmic battle. This cosmic battle breaks out between the archangel Michael and his angels against the dragon and his angels. The seer then identifies the dragon for the reader as follows: "The great dragon was thrown down, that ancient serpent, who is called the Devil and Satan, the deceiver of the whole world—he was thrown down to the earth, and his angels were thrown down with him." (Rev. 12:9). After Jesus has ascended to the throne and Satan has been defeated, he is then left to afflict the Christians: "Then the dragon was angry with the woman, and went off to make war on the rest of her children, those who keep the commandments of God and hold the testimony of Jesus." (Rev. 12:17)

It is in chapter 20 of the book that John describes the final defeat and destruction of Satan and his demons. An angel with the key to the bottomless pit descends and seizes the dragon (identified again as Satan), binding him first for 1,000 years (Rev. 20:1-3). At the end of that period of captivity, the angel then releases him once more to try to deceive the humans (Rev. 20:7-8). Then, in a final battle, God sends a fire to consume Satan's armies and throws him, along with a figure called the beast and the false prophet, into the lake of fire, where they will endure eternal torment (Rev. 20:9-10). This is also the eternal resting place of those individuals whose names are not found written in the book of life (Rev. 20:14-15).

The Apocalypse of Peter

Shortly after the book of Revelation was written, Christian writers authored another apocalyptic book that explored the nature of hell. This book did not make it into the final canon of scripture, but such notable figures as Clement of Alexandria (ca. 150-215) believed that it should be included in the Christian canon.

The Apocalypse begins with a final gathering of humanity before the throne of God for judgment. As is typical in these scenes, the righteous and the wicked are separated from each other. The author then begins to describe the fire of hell in excruciating detail:

> "...cataracts of fire shall be let loose; and obscurity and darkness shall come up and cover and veil the entire world, and the waters shall be changed and transformed into coals of fire, and all that is in it shall burn and the sea shall become fire; under the heaven there shall be a fierce fire that shall not be put out and it flows for the judgment of wrath. And the stars shall be melted by flames of fire, as if they had not been created." (Apoc. Pet. 5; Müller, 1992, 627)

The text goes on to describe individuals receiving punishment according to their sins. Women who braided their hair for the purposes of attracting men to sleep with them will be hung by their hair. Similarly, the men whom they slept with will be hung by their thighs (likely a euphemism for their genitals). The text lists a multitude of tortures and punishments for sinners. Loan sharks are thrown into a vat of excrement up to their knees. Disobedient children hang beside flesh-eating birds, and disobedient slaves chew their tongues off. It is in the Apocalypse of Peter that the idea of Satan and the demons as tormentors becomes full-blown.

The Birth of Lucifer

Gustave Dore's illustration of Lucifer and the Archangel Gabriel

The early Christian theologian Origen took the ideas developed in the Book of the Watchers and transformed them. Whereas the Jewish traditions had identified the fallen angels with the Nephilim in the book of Genesis, Origen identified Satan with the primordial gods and monsters that were alluded to by Job and the prophets. For Origen, the term "morning star" that appeared in Jerome's Latin translation of the Bible as "Lucifer" was to be identified with Satan, as was the "Prince of Tyre" mentioned in Ezekiel (Russell, 1981, 131). No longer were these prophetic passages allusions to a Canaanite myth but descriptions of Satan himself. Origen even associated Leviathan with Satan. Leviathan was a primordial sea monster that had its origins in a different Canaanite myth and was referenced in the book of Job (41:1-2).

Gustave Dore's engraving depicting the destruction of Leviathan

Having made these connections, Origen then retold the origin myth of Satan and his demons as follows. Satan was created along with the angels long before the creation of the physical universe. This contrasted with the previous Jewish tradition that situated the creation of the angels on day two of the seven day creation account in Genesis. Satan and his demons, who were all angels at the time, rebelled against God. Thus, according to Origen, it was not lust for human women that caused this group of angels to fall but rather the sin of pride.

The Christian church has generally fallowed Origen's narrative with respect to Satan, the Devil, and now Lucifer, ever since. The medieval depictions of Satan in art and literature all rely on this general narrative as the backdrop for their work.

The Physical Features of the Devil

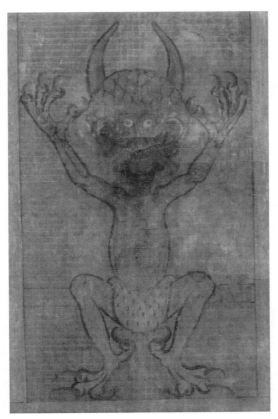

Depiction of the Devil in the Codex Gigas

Depictions of the devil in art became quite a common motif in the Middle Ages, and there are several physiological characteristics that become standard in such depictions. These standard features include a pair of horns, cloven hooves, a tail, a goatee, and the brandishing of a pitchfork. Wray and Mobley suggest that the idea of Satan possessing a horn and a tail relates to the Canaanite underworld demon Habayu, who appears in Ugaritic texts with these features (Wray & Mobley, 2005, 81), but making that connection probably goes too far given the nature of the evidence, because horns do not begin to appear in artistic portrayals of the devil until the 11th century A.D. The notion that an obscure figure who appears briefly in Ugaritic texts from the 12th century B.C. influenced Western artists living over 2,000 years later is preposterous.

This idea becomes even more farfetched when considering what were almost certainly the actual sources of these features. Medieval artists often looked to classical art for inspiration, especially art associated with Ancient Greek mythology. In Greek mythology, Hermes is the god who leads the dead to the underworld. The son of Hermes was Pan. Both Pan and Hermes were represented by phallic symbols, and one of the primary functions of the devil in the medieval literature was sexual temptation. Artistic portrayals of Pan show him with horns, cloven hooves, a tail and a goatee (Burton, 1984, 68). In many cases, the only way to differentiate between depictions of Pan and those of the devil is based on the items they carry. Pan most often carries a set of musical pipes, whereas the devil more often carries a pitchfork.

Ancient statue of Pan and a shepherd

The concept that the devil would carry something that would identify him was a natural extension of the fact that virtually all deities in classical art had symbols they carried to make them easily recognizable. The medieval artists most likely considered using various symbols for the devil, but in the end they decided to co-opt Poseidon's trident as a pitchfork that the devil would use to prod and torture his victims in hell.

Bibliography

Bailey, Lloyd R. "Enigmatic Bible Passages: Gehenna: The Topography of Hell." *The*

Biblical Archaeologist 49 (1986) 187-91.

Cumont, Franz. *Lux Perpetua*. Paris, 1949.

Herrmann, W. "Baal zebub." Pp. 154-56 in Karel van der Toorn, Bob Becking, and Pieter
    Willem van der Horst (eds.) *Dictionary of Deities and Demons in the Bible*. 2nd
    ed. Leiden, 1999.

Kyrtatas, Dimitris J. "The Origins of Christian Hell." *Numen* 56 (2009) 282-97.

Liddell, Henry G. and Robert Scott. *Greek-English Lexicon*. Abridged Addition. Oxford,
    1994.

Müller, C. Detlef G. "Apocalypse of Peter." Pp. 620-38 in Wilhelm Schneemelcher (ed.)
    New Testament Apocrypha. Vol. II. Louisville, KY, 1992.

Page, Hugh Rowland, Jr. *The Astral Revolt: A Study of its Reflexes in Canaanite and
    Hebrew Literature*. Unpublished Dissertation. Harvard University, 1990.

Pagels, Elaine. *The Origin of Satan*. New York, 1995.

Pietersma, Albert and Benjamin Wright. *A New English Translation of the Septuagint*.
    Oxford, 2007.

Riley, Greg J. "Devil." Pp. 244-49 in Karel van der Toorn, Bob Becking, and Pieter
    Willem van der Horst (eds.) *Dictionary of Deities and Demons in the Bible*. 2nd
    ed. Leiden, 1999.

Russell, Jeffrey B. *The Devil: Perceptions of Evil from Antiquity to Primitive
    Christianity*. Ithaca, 1977.

Russell, Jeffrey B. *Satan: The Early Christian Tradition*. Ithaca, 1981.

Russell, Jeffrey B. *Lucifer: The Devil in the Middle Ages*. Ithaca, 1984.

Stokes, Ryan E. "The Devil Made Me Do It...Or Did He? The Nature, Identity, and

Literary Origins of the Satan in 1 Chronicles 21:1." *Journal of Biblical Literature* 128 (2009) 91-106.

Watson, Duane F. "Gehenna." Vol II pp. 926-28 in David Noel Freedman (ed.) *The Anchor Bible Dictionary*. 6 vols. New York, 1992.

Wray, T. J. and Gregory Mobley. *The Birth of Satan: Tracing the Devil's Biblical Roots*. New York, 2005.

[i] Harvard excavations in the Punic city of Carthage that found dedicatory inscriptions (tombstones) and corresponding infant human remains suggest that such practices were not simply the rhetorical exaggerations of competing religious groups.

[ii] The one exception that Stausberg notes appears in a Middle Persian text (Ardā Vīrāz Nāmag) that another scholar (Tardieu) has clearly shown is full of Greek and Christian influences rather than the other way around.

Made in United States
North Haven, CT
31 August 2023

40974825R00028